HARLEY-DAVIDSON
THE LEGEND
GRANT LEONARD

**CHARTWELL
BOOKS, INC.**

Published by
CHARTWELL BOOKS, INC.
A Division of BOOKSALES, INC
PO Box 7100
114 Northfield Avenue, Edison
New Jersey 08818-7100

Produced by
Saturn Books Ltd
Kiln House, 210 New Kings Road
London SW6 4NZ

ISBN 1-55521-862-8

Reprinted 1994, 1995, 1996

Printed in China

PREVIOUS PAGE: *An
FXRS 1990 Low Rider.*

THESE PAGES: *An
FXRS-5P 1992 Sport Glide.*

CONTENTS

The Silent Gray Fellow

Harley hits the road

The story began in 1903 in a shed in the garden of the Milwaukee home of one Arthur Davidson, friend and partner of the young, bright Bill Harley. What came out of that shed was no more than a reinforced bicycle chassis powered by a simple De Dion-type single cylinder four-stroke motor. This dreadful popping and gasping boneshaker was the precursor of all Harley-Davidson motorcycles.

By 1909, the new Harley-Davidson motorcycle had gained some local notoriety, the orders were growing and the small group of fanatical owners of Harley's and Davidson's creation had given it a name – the Silent Gray Fellow. 'Silent' for its whispering exhaust note (an extremely modest approach to a motorcycle in its day) and the equally modest 'any color as long as it's gray' of the young designers. The 'Fellow' part we assume is the earliest recognition that Harley and Davidson built a reliable motorcycle of strong character – a bike to be trusted, an adventurer's friend.

It was officially designated the 5.35 and managed four horsepower from its 35ci displacement. Fifty miles per

ABOVE: *Simply gray – Harley's famous single earned a reputation for ruggedness and reliability.*

This example proves the point – it first burst into life way back in 1914.

hour was enough to scare even the bravest on the rudimentary and rutted roads of the day. In a nod to road-holding and civility, Bill Harley fitted the bike with girder forks and a sprung saddle.

The cylinder bore was $3\frac{5}{16}$ths of an inch with a stroke of 4 inches. Until 1919 it used an atmospheric induction system which meant the inlet valve opened on the downstroke simply due to the suction created by the falling piston. Final drive was by leather belt with a lever to disengage drive, in lieu of a clutch.

By 1918 the model had lost its appeal, swept aside by a new and enduring power in American motorcycling – the V-twin engine. Bill Harley made his first twin in 1909 by the simple addition of a second cylinder set at 45 degrees to the single pot of the Silent Gray Fellow. From that moment, Harley-Davidson's association with the V-twin motor was written in stone.

61F

The shape of things to come

Adding a second cylinder to their motor not only doubled the cubic capacity, but also the popularity of the Harley-Davidson. Once the American public had been treated to the sensation of the stomach-churning urge of the torquey V-twin motor, there was no going back. The Milwaukee motorcycle company's earliest successful design with this configuration was the 61F.

The 61 was state-of-the-art motorcycling. In 1912 Bill Harley designed and fitted a clutch into the rear hub. Not only did this make stop-starting a less hazardous affair, it allowed Harley to use a chain and cog to re-place the direct leather belt and pulley drive. Further-more, it made the fitting of a kick-start possible, an in-novation which would only be superseded in 1965 by electric start with the advent of the Electra Glide. The pushrods, cams and rockers were designed into the motor for the first time, too, with a new Intake Over Ex-haust (or 'pocket valve') system of positive valve actua-tion as standard.

Above all, the 61F was the machine which signaled the end of the days of quirky motorized bicycles for Har-ley-Davidson. This was Harley's first true purpose-built, blue-printed and designed motorcycle – a new breed of transport, and a sport and hobby in itself.

ABOVE AND BELOW: *Vee-power! Harley's first full production twin, the 61 cubic inch Model 11F. This one is from 1915. The motor is a 45-degree V-twin, a new idea then, but an 80-year-old tradition today.*

74JD Streamliner

A refined motorcycle

The design department of the Harley-Davidson factory concentrated much of its Great War-effort into refining one model – the 74J. New markets were opening up everywhere and the company needed to show the world a quality and reliable product.

The 74J motor was fundamentally the 61F, bored out to 74ci (1200cc from 1000cc). In a tooth and nail fight for domestic sales with arch-rival Indian, the bike received a thorough makeover in 1925. The frame was redesigned, positioning the motor lower down and utilizing it as a semi-stressed part of the chassis. The bike was redrawn with smoother and more rounded lines giving it the 'Streamliner' monicker. In its final update, battery and generator were introduced, doing away with the acetylene lamps used until then.

Comfort was a big selling point – this was a machine capable of sustained travel. It had robust, fat tires. The seat was 'Ful-Floteing,' with a sliding post which was spring-loaded in the rear frame downtube. It was low too, encouraging not only the male adventurers, but also one or two intrepid lady customers to throw a silk-clad leg over the J-model.

It was a machine which established the name Harley-Davidson worldwide and entrenched the marque in its own domestic market so firmly that it would ride the Great Depression and set up the company for a second great war-effort.

RIGHT: *Motorcycle luxury, 1920s-style. The thin and slabby gray look of the 61F is replaced by sexy curves and olive green with the Streamliner. This fine example made it all the way from 1927 to 1991, when it was snapped at Daytona Bike Week.*

61E Knucklehead

The idea of a Harley-Davidson holding any kind of speed record is, to the modern motorcyclist, something of a joke. Fastest to do what? Break down? Empty your wallet? In fact, back in 1936, the Harley-Davidson was considered by bikers around the world to be hot stuff. Indeed Harley-Davidson's new model for 1936 was vaunted as the fastest two wheeler in America. It was the 'Knucklehead' – and it packed quite a punch!

In a ploy to give the new model notoriety and get one over on the 'Wigwam' (the Indian factory), development rider and top Harley racer Joe Petrali took a prototype to Daytona beach and covered the flying mile at a world-record breaking speed of 136mph.

The machine he was hanging on to as he flew across the beach was powered by Harley's new overhead valve engine. It was the lumpy shape of the shiny rocker covers which gave the engine its 'Knucklehead' name. The new motor was 61ci (1000cc), had dry sump lubrication (marking the end of the total loss system) and a four-speed constant mesh gearbox. It was all housed in a 600lb double cradle framed chassis. In full road trim, the Knuckle would pull 90mph – about the same as a Harley of today. This basic specification of the 61E would endure for another 50 years of production.

THESE PAGES: *In 1936, the overhead valve Knucklehead was Harley's most powerful and fastest creation to date. Below, the famous Joe Petrali knuckles down to some serious speed-testing. The streamlining shown was actually removed for the 136mph record-breaking run as it was causing the bike to aviate as it scorched across Daytona Beach.*

Peashooter 21ci Single

The baby Harley

Since the Silent Gray Fellow, Harley owners have always seen it as their prerogative to nickname the new models from Milwaukee – to Harley's detriment as well as to their good. When the 21 cube (350cc) single cylinder lightweight came along, the tough big-vee boys couldn't resist a jibe. Next to the heavy guns, it truly was a Peashooter.

It flopped when it was launched in 1925. Forty-five miles per hour impressed nobody. Even in those days the American public had made up its mind – if it ain't a twin it ain't worth shoot. The original motor was a side-valve but was soon updated with overhead valves and a tune-up to give it another 20mph. In this guise it found its *raison d'être* – racing. On the dirt tracks and hill-climbs its revvy motor and light chassis gave it the potential to blast the rest into the weeds. And it did.

Factory rider Joe Petrali was unbeatable on his works bike, winning the 1935 National Hillclimbing Championship and the Grand Slam – all 13 American Motor-cycle Association National Championship rounds of the US dirt track championship.

It wasn't just the brilliance of Petrali which made the name of this diminutive machine; it was a winner around the world. Until, that is, a British marque by the name of JAP produced a more powerful motor than that of the Peashooter. Its run of success was at an end – but no-one mourned its passing; showroom sales, not race wins, were what counted then and Harley-Davidson had already ceased production of the little single in 1934.

BELOW: 'Peashooter' was an unlikely nickname for what became a red-hot race bike. The Peashooter dominated dirt ovals, near-vertical hillclimbs, and the road endurance races.

74UL/80ULH

Old faithful

The U-models typify the old Harley-Davidson approach to motorcycle marketing – not so much conservative, as backward. The OHV 61E Knucklehead had been a hit (despite teething problems) and won its place in history as a classic. Rather than building on this success, the factory's next move, in 1937, was to crank out a couple of dinosaurs – the 74UL and the bigger-than-ever 80ULH.

They were side-valve engines fitted to a similar chassis to the 61E, with circulated lubrication and dry sump. Two 600lb monsters, with 30hp motors which chugged like steam-trains, were an instant hit – just what America wanted! Who needs leaky, peaky overhead valves anyway?

Harley had satisfied the sporting clubmen with the hotshot 61E. Now they were taking care of the bread and butter business – the police forces, the family with bike

ABOVE: *An original super-reliable and super-grunty 1936 80ULH, on display in the Rodney C Gott museum at the Harley factory in York, Penn.*

and sidecar and the touring clubman. If they hadn't, the loyal Harley-man would no doubt have been forced to buy Indian.

The U models were simple, rugged, and reliable – the Model T Ford of the Harley-Davidson line-up. Harley had plugged a short-term gap in their own range, denying the rival Indian factory a precious market share.

The future could only lie with the power-efficient overhead valve system, however. And indeed, from 1941, Harley-Davidson would concentrate its war effort in that direction, finally putting the workhorse 80ULH with its grunty sidevalve motor out to pasture.

The 45

Hell on wheels

Like several Harley classics, the 45 began life as a sales disaster. Although it was launched on the brink of the Great Depression in 1929, Harley-Davidson was as much responsible for the flop as the economic climate. The 45ci sidevalve was underpowered and wasn't adequately tested as a prototype, with early models suffering generator drive shaft failure.

How did it become a classic? Just by hanging in there, and having its problems ironed out on the production line. In 1931 the bike was redesigned with a new frame to match the new engine. The clutch and transmission were beefed up to produce a bike which could be relied on to last. The following year its main opponent in the market, the superior Indian 101 Scout, was discontinued leaving the 45 to dominate the middleweight market. In 1937 it was given a bigger tank, larger cooling fins and dry sump lubrication. By 1939, the bike was established as the definitive rugged and reliable middleweight motorcycle and had founded the basis for a new production racing class for 45ci bikes.

Adolf Hitler was responsible for the 45's worldwide success. His Luftwaffe spent 1940 carpet-bombing the industrial heartland of England, targeting steel factories, munitions works, and tank and aircraft manufacturers. It was a dense industrial area and the concentration of explosives which rained down night after night over the West Midlands also bombed flat the world's main source of motorcycles. As the rubble of the Triumph, Norton and BSA factories smoldered, so Harley-Davidson was gearing up for its biggest export drive ever. And spearheading Harley's war effort was the 45. As the war sucked in virtually every developed country in the world, so each country was introduced to Harley-Davidson motorcycles.

The 45 was kitted up to play a full role in the action. The bike was expected to perform as well in the Sahara as in Siberia. Besides being daubed in a fetching shade of drab green, the 45 had wide wheel rims fitted to take large knobbly tires, a steel sump guard bolted on, the compression ratio was lowered, and the barrels and heads given larger cooling fins to give the engine an easier time; the three-speed transmission was left exactly as it was, having proved itself more bulletproof than a Sherman tank.

During the six-year conflagration, Harley-Davidson sent 88,000 of their 'sons' into battle. Two-thirds of these were used in the Soviet push to Berlin – a motorized cavalry of Harley-Davidson motorcycles. One positive aspect of the war for Harley-Davidson was that its name was spread worldwide. The dependability of the 45WLA left an impression on servicemen which would survive the war. The demand for Harleys in the postwar years was easily met – 15,000 army surplus 45s were dumped on the American market in 1945 and many found their way to Europe, converted back to civilian specification.

ABOVE AND TOP RIGHT: *A 1942 45WLA, kitted out for war duty and one of 88,000 bikes which H-D sent into action. The rifle came as an optional extra.*

OPPOSITE: *The same bike in 1946, this time demobbed and wearing some rather smart civvies which certainly didn't come from Harley-Davidson's wardrobe.*

The Servi-Car

Three wheels on my wagon

The Servi-Car was the oddest Harley ever. It had an odd number of wheels – three – and enjoyed a phenomenal 42-year production run. It was, as its name suggests, a service vehicle, aimed at the commercial and governmental markets. It began life with a narrow market in mind – car franchises. Garages would use the Servi-Car to tow customers from home to the garages for servicing and back again. But the three-wheelers' potential was soon recognized by the police forces who used the Servi-Car for traffic duty.

It was a user-friendly machine, fitted with the dependable 45ci sidevalve engine attached to a car-type rear differential. The demand for Servi-Cars kept the old 45 motor in production two decades beyond its expected lifespan. The Servi-Car was easy and safe to drive, being inherently stable with a spacious trunk for tools, equipment or goods. Harley advertized a 500lb carrying capacity, making the Servi-Car a very real alternative to a motor car as a goods vehicle. It was simply too useful and economical to fail.

There are plenty of Servi-Cars surviving today and the model has become the expression of the customizer's sense of humor, with a 'rest-room' facility being one of the most popular types of conversion.

ABOVE AND LEFT: *The three-wheeler Servi-Car was in production from 1932 to 1974. Above, a Servi-Car on duty with the San Francisco Police Department. This is one of the last models and sports an Electra Glide front end. Note the capacious trunk, almost large enough to hold a suspect! Left is one of the first models – same motor, different chassis.*

XL55 Sportster
Rock 'n' rollin' Harley

The rock 'n' roll era had its rock 'n' roll motorbikes – the Harley-Davidson Sportster XL was one of them. While Elvis Presley was gyrating at number one in the music charts, the Harley Sportster was proving almost as popular on the streets. The bike filled a void in the Harley range and gave the teenage biker of the day an alternative to the hot British bikes dominating the scene – Triumph, BSA and Norton.

Since before the war, England had been building middleweight twins of excellence – lightweight, good handling and fast-as-you-dare with modern overhead valve engines. Harley-Davidson had nothing to match. The XL Sportster was based on the KH54, a sidevalve motor derived from the venerable 45. Although the racing versions of the KH would dominate American racing for the next decade and beyond, it proved to be a sluggish and unpopular roadbike and was dropped to make way for the XL. In some quarters hailed as a radical new motor, it was in typical Harley style, based heavily on the KH but with overhead valves and revised combustion chamber.

The Sportster XL55 has survived to the present day as the XLH Sportster 883 – the bargain Harley. It's the spearhead of the Harley range, the bike you can afford and the bike to get you hooked on Harley riding *and* racing. In 1988, Bill Davidson, son of design chief Willie G Davidson, pulled an unlikely but clever marketing stunt by starting a one-make race series specially for the Sportster, putting Harley back on the racing scene and proving that the bike fully deserves its name.

ABOVE: *An Evolution Sportster 883 from 1989. It was the entry-level Harley – cheap and extremely cheerful.*

LEFT: *A Sportster 1000 'Hugger' built while Harley was owned by AMF in 1979.*

The Hydra Glide

Harley take the plunge

Harley-Davidson has never been accused of being innovative. Harley enthusiasts are such a conservative bunch it's more than the factory dares to try something radical. Sometimes, though, they just have to give in and go with the flow. This is what happened in 1949, when 40 years of leading link fork tradition was swept aside with the introduction of hydraulic telescopic forks. Harley must have been the last manufacturer in the world to accept this superior design of suspension.

The first bike they fitted telescopic forks to was their top-of-the-range tourer, the 74 FL. The bike, a big heavy beauty, was named the Hydra Glide, but the huge chromed shrouded forks, deeply vallanced fender and balloon tire made it look like a tank. The Hydra was also the first model to feature the Panhead motor – the rocker cover resembled an inverted saucepan.

The Harley fraternity never quite got over the imposition of telescopic forks. Thirty-six years later, in 1985, the factory launched the Springer Softail, which was fitted with leading link forks. It was seen as a gimmick by the modern biker, of course. Those traditionalists who were still alive to remember took it another way: after all these years it was an apology for the Hydra Glide.

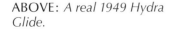

ABOVE: *A real 1949 Hydra Glide.*

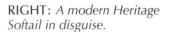

RIGHT: *A modern Heritage Softail in disguise.*

The Duo Glide
Springtime for Harley

THESE PAGES: *Harley don't like to shock their customers. When they introduced the two shock absorbers and swingarm on the 1958 Duo Glide, they were undoubtedly the last motorcycle manufacturer in the world to accept that rear suspension is a good idea after all.*

Progress was dragging Harley-Davidson screaming into the sixties. Across the Atlantic the English motorcycle industry was at its height. There wasn't a model on sale in Britain which didn't have some sort of rear suspension. Harley-Davidson still had a rigid rear-end on their big tourers. To compete with the likes of the Triumph Speed Twin, Harley had experimented with rear shock absorbers on their new hit model, the Sportster XL55. It seemed like a good idea.

Presented with the Duo Glide, the new top model tourer, with its new-fangled swinging fork and twin suspension units at the rear, traditionalists had just one question of the factory: 'Why?' Even the press of the day was critical of the new bouncy back-end. Surely it would soak up power and diminish traction? Surely the sprung seat and balloon tires could take care of rider comfort well enough? Those funny metal tubes just cluttered the back end.

Again, 30 years on, an apology in the form of the Softail was introduced, a modern Harley which glorified the rigid rear-end.

The Electra Glide

The world's most famous motorcycle

Ask anyone what an Electra Glide is and they'll tell you it's a motorcycle. They may not know what kind of motorcycle, but at least they know that much. Electra Glide is the most charistmatic name ever given to a bike. It sticks in the mind, it's a clever juxtaposition of two highly evocative words. With a name like that, whatever it is, it must be the best motorcycle in the world that money can buy.

Having a successful movie – *Electra Glide in Blue*, starring Robert Blake – carrying the enigmatic name helps spread the myth of the world's most desirable motorcycle. But legends aside, it was actually just a Duo Glide with an electric starter motor. In 1965 when the model was launched, electric start was still considered a luxury, though not unusual, on new bikes of the day. The Electra Glide was (and is) Harley's most luxurious model in every respect.

Since 1965, the model has been retained in the Harley line-up. Today, the Electra Glide Classic is the touring king. It is fitted with an enormous top-box, panniers and has stereo hi-fi as standard. It has a 1340cc (80ci) motor, is oil tight and reliable, and has maintenance-free belt drive. It'll cruise all day at a very acceptable 80mph, with the rider and pillion enjoying armchair comfort. Harley-Davidson call it the 'King of the Highway.' Long may it continue to reign.

RIGHT: *Scene from the film of the bike. It was always his dream to own an Electra Glide – a blue one. The inset picture shows someone else's electric blue dream – a customized Shovelhead. The main picture shows how much fun law enforcement can be.*

Super Glide FX1200
The Factory Chopper

The FX1200 remains one of the milestone models in Harley's history. Its evolution has been slow, conservative and methodical. The FX1200 Super Glide was a truly significant model, but not in itself. It was a signal that Harley-Davidson's marketing philosophy was taking a new road.

Since the mid-fifties, particularly in California, Harley fanatics have been customizing their bikes, adapting and enhancing them to suit their taste and to express their own individuality. Back then, Harley-Davidson, was extremely sensitive about its association with outlaw motorcycle gangs and a drop-out subculture which had adopted the Harley as a means of self-expression. As Harley saw it, there was overlap between the two types of biker, but they weren't one and the same.

By the seventies, a whole international industry had grown around customizing Harleys. Willie G Davidson, grandson of founder Arthur Davidson's brother, William, had been on the road meeting Harley folk around the States. He soon discovered that outlaw bikers were just a tiny element of a huge Harley culture which had grown up. To his surprise, he found that his

THESE PAGES: Willie G Davidson, of Milwaukee's first family, is the Chief of Design at Harley-Davidson.

His first project was the FX1200 – Harley's first factory custom.

family's products had become revered symbols of freedom and patriotism among this subculture, certainly nothing to be ashamed of. And he realized Harley-Davidson was completely out of touch with its market. As Chief of Styling, he was in the best position to do something about it.

The Super Glide, then, was Harley's first factory custom. Like the stripped minimalist big-inch hogs he came across on his travels, the FX1200 was Harley's largest 'touring' motor in a bare chassis with a skinny Sportster front end. The Super Glide was a high-profile, macho, boulevard cruiser and nothing else. Style for the sake of style, wrapped up in patriotic colors of 'Sparkling America' – red, white and blue. And it was the keystone of Harley-Davidson's future.

KR750

Flat heads and no brakes

Much of American motorcycle racing takes place in the dirt. And Harley-Davidson have always been right there, kicking it in everyone's face. The KR750 was Harley's production racer. It was a multi-faceted machine, adaptable for everything from the short track, half-mile and mile dirt oval, to road races and even the Daytona Speedway.

It was based on a middleweight roadbike, the K45 – a 45ci (750cc) sidevalve unit engine with the distinctive 'flat' cylinder heads, hence the monicker, 'flathead.' The bike was launched in 1952, 13 years after Triumph had launched their super-successful (and faster) overhead valve 500cc Speed Twin. Harley were sticking to what they knew best and could produce more cheaply. Adventurous, they were not.

Fortunately for the factory, the Harley-dominated governing body of racing, the American Motorcycle Association, moved the goalposts by banning overhead valve machines of over 500cc from the national championship, thereby validating the KR despite its obsolete technology.

The racing, however, was extremely exciting. With everyone given similar machines and the Brits having to try that much harder, the competition was hot. For dirt

use, the KR could be converted to a rigid rear end (then considered appropriate for dirt racing) by bolting on a rear subframe, or it could be fitted with shock absorbers for roadracing. An infinite combination of gear ratios was available for the four-speed box. Drum brakes could also be fitted (unnecessary on dirt bikes, but strongly advised on racers), as could fairings and different sized wheels.

The beauty of this one-model racing was that factory-backed riders weren't necessarily at an advantage. There's only so much you can do to a sidevalve twin within the rules, and there were many private tuners as capable as the factory experts. Champions were champions by rider ability at the highest level.

The KR750 was king of the tracks for 18 years, be-tween 1952 and 1970. In that time the engine was developed from around 38 horsepower to around 65 horsepower – a private as much as an official effort. In those 18 years, the national championship was won by privateers eight times, by factory riders five times and by British makes five times. It was a classic era of American motorcycle racing. Cal Rayborn had won Daytona in 1968 averaging over 100mph. Harley won 18 out of 23 Nationals in the same year. Harley's huge success ended abruptly in 1969 when, under pressure from the foreign lobby, the AMA finally changed the equivalency rule. A year later Harley's new overhead valve production racer was launched – the XR750. But the moment the floodgates opened, the British and Japanese took over.

LEFT: *A road racing KR750, in café-race trim with a cute nose fairing. They came from the factory with full streamlining.*

ABOVE: *A KR750 dirt-tracker shows off its fine lines.*

XR750

A hog in the limelight

The XR750 was the first attempt at replacing the KR flat-head. It was a panic move, a half-baked, sleeved-down Sportster which the racing department threw together to be ready for the 1970 racing season. It blew up.

Back to the drawing board and two years later a more durable product was packed off to the dealers. This was a ground-upwards redesign, but a 45-degree vee-twin, of course. It was still based on the Sportster, but was a radical Harley nonetheless. Today, the bike and certainly engines are still in sporadic production (although principally as a spares and advice back-up service) and it's still winning races on its own home-ground dirt ovals.

The XR was the first Harley to have an oversquare (stroke shorter than bore) engine at 3.125-inches bore by 2.98-inches stroke. The cases and top end are all of light but strong alloy; it runs with dual plugs in the head and two 40mm Mikuni flatslide carbs. The clutch runs dry and the gearbox has four speeds. The motor has 100bhp potential – if you want to win you have to find it yourself! The real key to success, however, is in achieving the power with reliability. The bikes are tuned for flat, high torque delivered over a wide spread, which is what's needed to get traction in the dirt on the big oval tracks. It's why the Harleys are still there; high horsepower is all very well, but if it's just spinning the back wheel you won't be going anywhere.

One notorious XR750 rider used to find traction even in mid-air. Stuntman Evel Knievel broke every bone in his body crashing his XR750 from on high. For Harley, the crazy leaps of Knievel brought worldwide attention to the flying bike.

The XR has been raced on asphalt tracks, fully faired with clip-on bars mainly in Battle of the Twins races, but the Japanese high-tech, high-revving motors don't show the old Harleys much mercy. Daytona has been the scene of Harley success in recent years, but with a slightly different version of the XR.

THESE PAGES: *Perhaps the most versatile production racer ever made, the XR came in both dirt and asphalt track trim.*

Aermacchi Harley-Davidson 250/350

Italian cousins

Harley-Davidson has four full world championships to its credit, though it's not something the factory brags about too loudly. The reason is that the bikes were designed, made, tuned, and race-prepared in Italy. And ridden by an Italian – Walter Villa.

In 1960 Harley-Davidson bought a half-share in the small Italian Aermacchi factory in Varese, near Milan. They produced lightweight two-stroke and four-stroke bikes. Italians being Italians, they were extremely keen on racing their products and had success in 1966 with the great Renzo Pasolini taking a third in the 350cc World Championship.

By the early seventies, the factory had developed a bike which would carve them a large niche in racing history. It used a two-stroke, parallel twin-cylinder motor, watercooled and with a dry clutch. The bike seemed to be invincible, winning three 250cc World Championships in three successive years from 1974 to 1976. Rider Walter Villa scored a double in 1976 by winning the 350cc Championship, too.

At the time, the Japanese dominated the two-stroke market worldwide and were deeply committed to racing. The Italian Harley-Davidson had them beat. Back home though, Harley were almost embarrassed by this racing success, as the sales success of the company was by no means as impressive. In 1978, Harley closed the factory down: they built big twins, not buzzing two-strokes.

LEFT: *Walter Villa, the 1977 reigning 250 and 350cc World Champion, racing the 250cc Harley-Davidson at the Belgian Grand Prix. Harley didn't know whether to be proud or embarrassed at the fantastic success.*

INSET: *The four stroke single, A la Verde 250cc Sprint. This was the lightweight bike which Harley hoped would be a poke in the eye for the British marques which dominated the small-capacity market.*

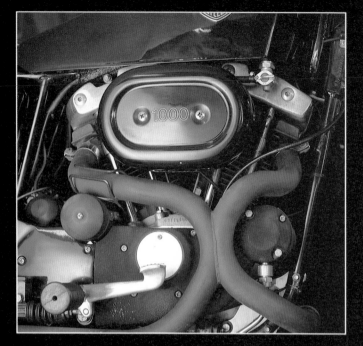

XLCR1000 Café Racer

Black, strong, and sweet

Why is it that so often collector's bikes start life as show-room lepers? Willie G Davidson's personal market research told him that the punters out there were into café racers: stripped, low, pseudo-race track machines for Sunday sprints to the next coffee bar. They were usually Japanese bikes or old British iron for credibility. Harley should give them what they want.

The XL Sportster was the starting point. The new bike was given an XR-style frame, with box-section swing-arm for added strength. The motor was the Sportster XL1000, blacked-up; it had a neat siamese exhaust, twin discs at the front and seven-spoke cast wheels. A small headlamp cowl fairing was fitted, and a slabby long tank which joined an XR750-style seat. Everything was painted black. It had to look mean.

The pre-publicity garnered great interest; dealers ordered in dozens. In 1977 2000 were made and 1200 the year after. But the bike didn't move. It was a lemon. The public weren't interested. Willie G had shot himself in the foot. His design and marketing ideas had so far been good and his factory choppers were a great success, but they further served to niche Harley-Davidson into its 'bad-boy' image. To the Triumph/Kawasaki-mounted ton-up boys, a café-racer Harley was a contradiction in terms – a rolling joke.

Ironically, the XLCR was a great improvement over the standard XL, with better rear suspension, a more ergonomic riding position and a more sensibly large gas tank. But when did practicality ever sell a Harley?

THESE PAGES: *The XLCR was the bike that nobody understood. In an era when the Harley-Davidson image had crystallized as the easy rider's machine, Willie G popped up with a street racer. Next to the Japanese wonderbikes, the Café Racer's underwhelming performance could only serve to embarrass its rider.*

XR1000

The fastest in the west

As the XR750 barreled around the dirt tracks of America building an enviable reputation as a macho muscle winner, it occurred to Harley-Davidson that a road-going version of the production racer couldn't fail to capture the imagination of the power-hungry, patriotic, aspiring Jay Springsteens in the market.

In 1983, they announced the XR1000, a big-bore, rip-roaring hot-rod motorcycle. The dealers went wild, the public began to rattle their cages. Harley-Davidson were so taken aback by the instant rapturous reaction that they upped the retail price by a couple of grand, convinced they were on to a sure winner.

Unfortunately, the public's expectation of what was to come, wasn't quite met. Far from it. It wasn't a bored-out XR750 which was on offer here. The bike only had the power of a well-serviced XL1000 Sportster. And the word went out quickly. So quickly in fact, that it killed the model stone dead. Seven thousand dollars for the same performance of a bike half the price? No thanks.

Harley-Davidson didn't quite play their cards right. They had contracted Jerry Branch, famed Harley tuner and ex-factory man, to prepare the heads and design a tuning kit to sell with the bike for an extra $1000. Such was the disappointment in the XR1000 that few made the extra investment. Which was a shame, as Branch's kit would double the horsepower of the standard XR to around 100bhp! The promised hot-rod was there all-along, but just badly presented. This fact slowly came to light over the following years, creating collector interest in the model; its status was further enhanced in 1984 when Gene Church took an XR1000 called 'Lucifer's Hammer' to victory at Daytona in the Battle of the Twins race, a feat he repeated in 1985 and 1986.

LEFT: *Whoever Clyde Cranknuts is, he can sure build a nice custom XR1000.*

BELOW: *The slightly more standard-looking example. This beaut is not trying too hard to win a prize at Daytona's Rat's Hole show.*

FXRS Sport Glide

The Evolution revolution

In the late seventies, Harley-Davidson was at its lowest ebb. Now owned by a huge leisure conglomerate, AMF, Harley had soaked up millions in emergency investment, but decade after decade of tight-fisted and conservative management had left Harley outside any commercial reality. They had no direction, the Japanese were flooding the market with far superior machinery and the old Milwaukee Vee seemed to all like a sad anachronism. Worse, it was notoriously unreliable. One well-known saying was: 'Buy a Harley, buy the best, ride a mile and walk the rest!'

AMF tried to sell the business in 1980. They got one serious offer – from the management. By 1981, the management buy-out group was in charge, with Vaughn Beals as Chairman, and they set about rebuilding the Harley business.

The foundation of the phenomenal recovery of Harley-Davidson is the Evolution V2 engine. How something so different could look so similar is a mystery, but the key to the new age of Harley was the bike's reliability and high quality construction. Yet it sacrificed none of its distinctive Harley character. This clever mix of new and old – new methods, old style – was the new theme for Harley-Davidson. The stigma of breakdowns, oil leaks and component failure was quickly forgotten. It was the product of a complete revision of working methods at the Harley plants; they had much to thank the Japanese for.

The first of the new generation was the FXRS Sport Glide. It was a 1340cc (80-cube) motor, pushing out around 50bhp and 85ft-lb of torque. The motor was in large rubber mountings, effectively isolating the chassis from vibration – hence the instant nickname 'Rubber Glide.' Drive was by Gates belt made from Kevlar – a 40,000-mile component.

It took a while for this new product to sink into the consciousness of bikers and the motorcycle industry worldwide. Harley themselves helped it along by instigating a whole new policy of customer involvement through the Harley Owners Group and a design and marketing policy which could only have come from Willie G. It's unique in motorcycling, and for that matter, any other business. It was the deliberate development of the Harley legend through self-celebration and promotion. Over the next few years, the whole Harley-Davidson range would become a modernized reflection of old models from the postwar years and old customiz-

ing styles of the fifties and sixties. Customers were soon getting in line to buy a piece of the action.

Harley-Davidson's turnaround within the last decade has been the greatest motorcycling success story ever. Besides commercial success, Harley-Davidson has created something more. Its direct association and personal involvement with its customers is unique in motorcycling. When a person buys a Harley today, he or she buys into a whole lifestyle, a whole new social life. It's too attractive and fun to fail. It's the reason the 'bubble' will not burst for Harley-Davidson. Harley-Davidson isn't a fashion or a passing fancy – it's a way of life and everyone is welcome to join the band of Harley brothers, if they've got the price of membership.

LEFT: *The 1992 version of the bike which was the cornerstone of Harley-Davidson's phenomenal recovery during the 1980s. This particular example has a 'liberated' motor, with open pipes and Screamin' Eagle carburetor.*

ABOVE AND LEFT: *The reliable Evolution engine has all the torque of a truck. If you're talking performance, Harley-Davidson don't sell the bike on horsepower – which is just as well – they sell the stump-pullin' grunt.*

XLH883 Sportster

Everybody's favorite piglet

The Evolution-engined Sportster played a key role in the recovery of Harley-Davidson in the early eighties. It was their loss-leader. In motorcycle marketing, loss-leaders are often huge impressive flagship models. Harley looked at it another way. If they could get people on to and 'into' their motorcycles, they'd become customers forever. And with a shot reputation, they had a lot of faith to rebuild. In 1986 the entry model Harley was introduced: the brand new 883 Sportster priced at a cut-throat $3995.

The bike was a reflection of the Sportster introduced way back in 1952. It had all the looks and image, and was a solid, reliable little motorcycle. Harleys still had a reputation for being way overpriced, compared to the super-tech, fast, and reliable Japanese competition. You

had to be some enthusiast to buy one. Suddenly there was a Harley which was cheap beyond belief and was proving to be reliable.

It was an instant hit. Harley deliberately kept supply just below demand; it kept interest up and the second-hand market buoyant. The new Sportster was basic and simple; the modest 45bhp 883cc motor was solid-mounted, but smooth with it. It had a single disc brake at the front, a single clock to tell you it wasn't the fastest motor around. But it was only intended as a simple street cruiser. Indeed, simplicity was part of its attraction; it had a clean, lean look with its peanut tank, pillow seat and short dual shotgun exhausts. It all served to exaggerate the huge cylinders of the motor – that big 'vee' said Harley at a glance.

LEFT: *The Evolution Sportster 883's 1200cc big brother (below, far left) is almost identical but for its bigger pistons (and price tag!).*

BELOW: *The author riding the 1991 Harley 883 Sportster Championship-winning bike owned by Warr's of London. In race trim, the engine is tuned (within the rules) to produce 60bhp. The racing, nevertheless, is fast and furious.*

Heritage Softail

Let's do the time warp again

Another model with Willie G Davidson written all over it, the Heritage Softail of 1987, was the ultimate nostalgia styling job. The Hydra Glide of 1949 was the last hard-tail Harley and a classic with it. That was the style Willie G wanted reflected in his new bike. Hard-tail frames are *de rigeur* in the custom Harley world, but a bike with no rear suspension would be asking too much of the more delicate *derrières* of the general market. What they built then was a bike with no visible rear suspension. The rear part of the frame would swing, and two shock absorbers laid flat under the engine would sort out the damping. The Hydra Glide was reborn and named the Heritage Softail.

The Heritage Softail carried the Evolution 80ci motor, but unlike the FLH and FXR models, this one had to be bolted direct to the frame, lacking the luxury of rubber mounts. Vibration was not intrusive and even added a little to the character of the bike.

The Softail formed the basis for a new range of Harleys, all oozing nostalgia. The Heritage Softail Custom, with its studded leather saddlebags and fringed seat seemed to take the concept to its extreme; then they built the Springer.

The Springer Softail had the motorcycling world gasping in wonder — wonder at how Harley could be so audacious! Inspiration for this model went back to the prewar days. Harley turned their back on 40 years of suspension development and went back to the girder front fork. The bike was a sensation with girder forks and a hardtail look. It was certainly a visual success if not such a hit in terms of performance. Fork travel was short and sudden, and rather too much was expected of that skinny front tire. It was the model which demonstrated perfectly what the reborn Harley-Davidson was all about.

BELOW: *Spot the shocks? You can't because they're hidden, laid horizontally under the gearbox. The whole rear subframe pivots to allow wheel movement – the classic Hydra Glide* looks without sacrificing (much) comfort.

RIGHT: *The return of girder forks with the Springer Softail.*

Dyna Glide FXD1340

The all-American motorcycle

BELOW: *The second model to feature the Dyna chassis, the Daytona 50th Anniversary limited edition. It's styled like the last pre-Evolution engine 80-cube bikes featuring an 'invisible' frame. Very un-Japanese and attractive to traditionalists, apparently.*

RIGHT: *A pair of Dyna Glides at rest.*

The Dyna Glide chassis was introduced in 1990 in response to customer demand. The traditionalists of America never really took to the FXR chassis allegedly because, with its triangulated tubing around the sidepanels, it looked too Japanese. A new chassis was drawn up to form a new range of 1340 Low-Rider-style models.

While considering the Dyna chassis, Harley's design engineers set about giving the bike the look of the Hogs of the seventies – like the FX Super Glide, Willie G's first factory 'custom.' The triangulated tubing went and the battery box took its rightful place on the side of the bike. To do this, they moved the oil tank underneath the motor and relocated the filter at the front, both in more logical positions than on the FXR frame. The bike's electrics loom was rationalized too. Now the main junctions were collected in a nice accessible box in the middle of the bike, rather than being stuffed in the headlight, and the loom channeled inside the frame.

As for the ride, it handled as well as the FXR, but the forks were raked further, adding to the bike's high-speed stability with a slight forfeit in low-speed manageability. The first model with the chassis was the Sturgis, in sexy black with red decals, commemorating the Black Hills Sturgis rally.

The Ultra Glide

The ultimate ride

Harley-Davidson have always striven to give their touring clubmen a comfortable ride. In 1990 the factory built the most luxurious motorcycle ever – the Ultra Glide. It was based on the Electra Glide Classic, itself a comprehensively equipped motorcycle.

The Ultra Glide carried the 1340cc motor which allows a loping pace of 60mph with just a couple of thousand rpm and change on the tacho. Vibrations were totally isolated by the rubber mounts for the engine. It was a relaxing ride. The rider was protected from inclement weather (and hapless bugs) by a huge, wide handlebar fairing and leg shields. Besides a CB radio, built into the fairing was a stereo system which could blast out, perfectly audibly, at up to 85mph! Steppenwolf never sounded so good! Even the pillion had a couple of speakers in the arm rests. Arm rests? Yes and both riders and pillion enjoyed a fully padded backrest.

Long distant merchants had never had it so good. Luggage capacity was generous – the King Tour Pak trunk could hold three cases of beer, with room for a change of underwear. And if the trunk and panniers weren't enough, well you could always tow a trailer. Or fit a sidecar – the ultimate four-wheeled motorcycle. The dictionary defines ultra as 'beyond or surpassing a specified extent or range.' This Harley will take you as far as you want to go, and then a little farther.

THESE PAGES: *The Ultra Glide Classic is an activity center for adults. As standard, it's packed with gadgets from CB radio to stereo cassette player.*

Looking at the Ultra at standstill, you get the same feeling as looking at a Jumbo jet – how does something so enormous get off the ground?